CU00652157

Table of Contents

The Shadow of His Wings

A GRAPHIC BIOGRAPHY OF
FR. GEREON GOLDMANN

Ignatius.com

AugustineInstitute.org

The Shadow of His Wings

A GRAPHIC BIOGRAPHY

HILL 444. AS I REMEMBER, IT WAS THE MIDDLE OF 1943; OUR TROOPS HAD BEEN ORDERED INTO SICILY TO PROTECT THE RETREAT OF THE BADLY BEATEN REMNANT OF THE GERMAN ARMY.

THE HILL WAS CALLED 444 BECAUSE IT WAS 444 METERS HIGH. THE ENEMY WAS DUG IN. WE WERE COMMANDED TO TAKE THE HEIGHTS FROM THEM. IT WAS A FOOLISH, STUPID ORDER, CONSIDERING OUR LACK OF TROOP STRENGTH AND OUR SORRY EQUIPMENT.

THE NIGHT BEFORE THE ASSAULT, SOME COMPANIES WERE STILL WITHOUT OFFICERS. I GOT COMPANY 10.

THOUGH WE WERE FRESH TROOPS, FEW WERE EXPERIENCED SOLDIERS. EXCEPT MY AMBULANCE DRIVER FAULBORN AND ME, COMPANY 10 WAS MADE UP OF YOUNG STUDENTS TAKEN STRAIGHT FROM SCHOOL AND DRAFTED.

THE GREATER NUMBER OF THEM WERE UNDER TWENTY YEARS OF AGE; SOME WERE ONLY SIXTEEN OR SEVENTEEN. THESE HAD BEEN THE HITLER YOUTH.

THESE BOYS, IN ALL GOOD FAITH, WERE FIRED UP WITH ENTHUSIASM FOR THE GERMAN CAUSE.

HAVE YOU SEEN ANYONE DIE?

I'M SORRY, WHAT?

HAVE YOU SEEN ANYONE DIE?

9

ONLY SHORT LEAPS WERE POSSIBLE.

THUMP

BLOOD WAS FLOWING FROM HIS SHATTERED CHEST.

-KOFF KOFF- ...NOT NOW. KOFF

THOUGH WE TOOK THE HEIGHTS, OUR LOSSES WERE HEAVY.

THE COMMANDER

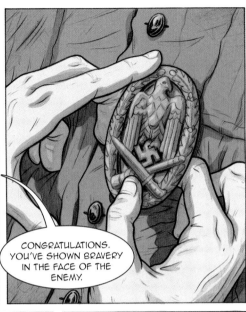

CONGRATULATIONS. YOU'VE SHOWN BRAVERY IN THE FACE OF THE ENEMY.

BUT I JUST RAN AS THE REST DID.

IT ISN'T OFTEN THAT A NON-COMBATANT SOLDIER RECEIVES SUCH A FIELD COMMISSION.

YES, WELL. I CANNOT DERIVE MUCH SATISFACTION IN RECEIVING THIS MEDAL.

THIS NEW COMMANDER DID NOT KNOW, BUT THROUGHOUT MY CAREER AS A NAZI I HAD FREQUENTLY REFUSED SIMILAR HONORS AND THE DOCTRINES THEY IMPLIED.

OF COURSE, THIS SORT OF IMPUDENCE COULD GET ME IN TROUBLE...

MAY, 1943

I RECEIVED NEWS THAT AN AIR ATTACK HAD DAMAGED THE HOME OF MY PARENTS. THIS BROUGHT MY LONG PROMISED, OFTEN-DEFERRED LEAVE OF ABSENCE, AND I WENT HOME TO FULDA.

I FOUND MYSELF WITH SOME SPARE TIME AND REALIZED I WAS IN FRONT OF THE CONVENT WHERE I HAD SERVED MY FIRST MASS AS AN ALTAR SERVER, NINETEEN YEARS EARLIER.

HELLO MY BOY...

SISTER!

SISTER SOLANA MAY, THE SACRISTAN WHO TAUGHT ME TO SERVE.

THERE IS-- THE WAR--

WAR? THE BIBLE DOES NOT SAY, "PRAYERS ARE ANSWERED EXCEPT DURING A FOOLISH WAR, IN WHICH EVENT GOD IS POWERLESS." DO YOU BELIEVE THAT GOD IS MIGHTIER THAN THE WAR?

OF COURSE I DO. BUT THE LAWS OF THE CHURCH; I DON'T--

THE MATTER IS VERY SIMPLE. YOU WILL SEE THE POPE. HE MADE THE LAWS, HE CAN ALSO DISPENSE FROM THEM.

TOMORROW MORNING I RETURN TO THE FRONT IN SICILY. THE POPE DOES NOT LIVE THERE, SISTER. BESIDES, WITHOUT MY STUDIES, HE WOULD NEVER ORDAIN ME A PRIEST.

HMM. YOU MUST PRAY TO THE MOTHER OF GOD IN LOURDES. THEN YOU WILL SEE THE POPE IN ROME. AND YOU MUST ASK HIM BOLDLY FOR YOUR ORDINATION.

SUCH CHILDLIKE FAITH--ALMOST CHILDISH FAITH.

THIS CONVERSATION CONTINUED FOR SOME TIME; I REMAINED RESOLVED THAT SISTER SOLANA MAY'S PREDICTION OF MY PRIESTHOOD WAS FOLLY. SHE WAS EQUALLY CONVINCED HER PRAYERS WOULD BE HEARD.

1924

SISTER SOLANA MAY THOUGHT I WOULD BE A PRIEST, BUT GIVEN MY REPUTATION WHILE GROWING UP IN FULDA, IT IS AMAZING THAT I EVEN BECAME A SEMINARIAN.

AS A BOY, I LED MY BROTHERS TO PLAY PLENTY OF TRICKS AND COMMIT MUCH MISCHIEF.

DESPITE OUR RUDENESS, OUR HOME LIFE WAS MARKED BY A DEEP FAITH AND TRUE PIETY. FATHER AND MOTHER WERE MODELS OF CATHOLIC PARENTS.

I THINK PERHAPS I WAS WILD, RATHER THAN BAD.

WHEN I WAS BORN, MY FATHER WAS IN MILITARY SERVICE ON THE WESTERN FRONT, BUT FOR MOST OF MY CHILDHOOD HE WORKED AS A VETERINARIAN.

WHEN HE LEARNED OF OUR MISCHIEF, FATHER WOULD GIVE US A SEVERE LESSON, WITH A ROD AS THE CHIEF TEACHING AID.

20

MY MOTHER WAS A TRULY AMAZING PERSON WITH A WEALTH OF UNDERSTANDING AND SYMPATHY.

HER KITCHEN WAS OFTEN OCCUPIED BY SOME TROUBLED WIFE FROM THE COUNTRYSIDE WHO HAD COME TO ASK HER ADVICE.

SHE WAS THE ONE WHO TAUGHT ME TO DEFEND THE SMALL AND THE WEAK, TO CONSOLE THE UNDERDOG, ESPECIALLY SINCE I WAS QUITE BIG AND STRONG.

SHE DIED WHEN I WAS EIGHT.

MANY HUNDREDS OF PEOPLE WHO HAD BEEN ATTRACTED TO HER KINDNESS ATTENDED THE BURIAL.

HER DEATH MARKED THE DARKEST DAY OF MY YOUTH.

I COULD NOT EXPLAIN BEING DETAINED.

I'D TAKEN ACTIONS AGAINST THE NAZIS, BUT IN PERFECT SECRET, OR WITH THE CONFIDENCE OF SOME HIGH RANKING AGITATOR.

LATER, I LEARNED FROM FAULBORN THAT DURING MY CAPTIVITY THE UNIT WAS DESTROYED IN SICILY. HE WAS ONE OF THE ONLY SURVIVORS.

YOU ARE TO BE RELEASED IMMEDIATELY.

SOMEONE IN BERLIN DISMISSED YOUR CHARGES. YOU'LL REJOIN YOUR DIVISION; FIRST YOU HAVE SPECIAL DUTIES IN FRANCE THOUGH.

WHAT?

WHERE?

LET'S SEE... PAU. DO YOU KNOW LOURDES? IT'S CLOSE BY.

BUT I DID NOT CONSIDER THAT THIS MYSTERIOUS ARREST MIGHT BE SPARING MY LIFE; I WORRIED IMPRISONMENT WOULD LAST FOREVER.

I WAS ABLE TO GO TO LOURDES A FEW DAYS LATER. PERHAPS SISTER SOLANA MAY'S FAITH WAS NOT SO CHILDISH.

THE BISHOP COULD NOT SPARE A PRIEST, BUT NOW I COULD DISTRIBUTE THE EUCHARIST. AND AFTER HE HEARD MY CONFESSION, I WAS PREPARED FOR MY NEW DUTY.

HE FORGAVE ME GRACIOUSLY. I THANKED LITTLE SISTER SOLANA FROM FULDA, WHO SEEMED TO HAVE WON THIS SPECIAL GRACE FOR ME BY HER PRAYERS.

WE DROVE BACK PAST THE ENGLISH GUNSHIPS TO OUR HIDING PLACE IN THE CLIFFS WHERE WE CARED FOR THE WOUNDED.

THAT SAME NIGHT I TOLD TWO RECENTLY INJURED MEN THEIR CONDITION WAS SERIOUS AND ASKED IF THEY WERE CATHOLIC.

ARE YOU A PRIEST?

NO, BUT I HAVE HOLY COMMUNION.

I PRAYED AN ACT OF CONTRITION WITH HIM AND GAVE HIM HOLY VIATICUM.

YOU SHOULD RECEIVE HOLY COMMUNION ALSO.

SUCH A PIECE OF BREAD WILL NOT SAVE ME. RATHER, PUT A CIGARETTE IN MY MOUTH.

I HAD MANY DISHEARTENING EXPERIENCES LIKE THIS AMONG THE NAZIS. STILL I HAD A PERSISTENT FEELING THAT EVERYTHING WOULD SOME HOW TURN OUT ALL RIGHT. I WAS NOT LIGHTHEARTED, BY ANY MEANS, BUT I WAS NOT AFRAID EITHER.

NOW THEY WERE BOTH BEFORE THE JUDGMENT SEAT OF GOD.

1928

I WAS INCORRIGIBLE UNTIL MY MOTHER'S DEATH.

BUT AFTER SHE DIED SISTER SOLANA MAY TOLD ME, "I WILL TAKE THE PLACE OF YOUR MOTHER."

EVEN WITH OUR NEW SPIRITUAL LEADERS, WE WERE UNRULY BOYS.

WITH NEW ENTHUSIASM FOR THE CHURCH, I JOINED THE BUND NEUDEUTSCHLAND YOUTH GROUP...

... BUT AS TIME PASSED, MY COUNTRY CAME UNDER THE DARK SPELL OF ADOLPH HITLER.

THE CHRISTIAN AND HITLER YOUTH GROUPS BECAME MORE AND MORE ANTAGONISTIC.

WE ENGAGED IN WHAT EVENTUALLY BECAME REAL BATTLES...

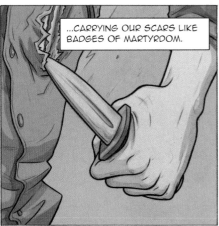

...CARRYING OUR SCARS LIKE BADGES OF MARTYRDOM.

WHEN THE POLICE ARRESTED AND IMPRISONED US, IT WAS PART OF THE ADVENTURE.

UNAWARE OF THE MORAL DANGER OR THE POLITICS...

...WE SIMPLY OPPOSED THE NAZIS AS OUR NATURAL ENEMIES.

SUDDENLY, I WOKE UP.

GET UP AND RUN! SCHNELL! THERE IS NO TIME TO WASTE!!

GET UP AND

A VOICE.

RUN IT IS PAST TIME!!

UM... BREAKFAST?

SET DOWN THE FOOD AND GET READY. WE NEED TO LEAVE NOW.

I HAVE NO TIME TO EXPLAIN IT TO YOU, BUT FOR THE SAKE OF YOUR WIFE AND CHILDREN, ROUSE THE OTHERS AND GATHER YOUR THINGS.

FAULBORN SEEMED MANIFESTLY IMPRESSED BY WHAT I SAID AND THE WAY IN WHICH I SAID IT.

32

WE NEED TO GET EVERYBODY BACK TO THE REST OF THE COMPANY RIGHT NOW.

THE BRIDGE IS STILL GUARDED BY THAT ENGLISH MACHINE-GUN EMPLACEMENT. RIGHT NOW THEY'RE SHOOTING THE MICE THAT TRY TO GET ACROSS THAT RIVER. WE'LL HEAD BACK ONCE THE ARMY MOVES.

NO. WE'LL FIND ANOTHER WAY; I CANNOT SAY WHY, BUT WE HAVE TO GO THIS INSTANT.

WE ROUSED THEM ALL, BUT THE OTHERS REFUSED TO COME.

THE ONLY REMAINING WAY TO REACH THE GERMAN LINES, WITHOUT USING THE BRIDGE, OR ALERTING THE WARSHIPS THAT GUARDED THE COAST, WAS THROUGH THIS WATER.

I AM NOT A GOOD SWIMMER

TRY NOT TO STEP OFF INTO THE DEEPS.

THE OBSCURITY OF THE EARLY MORNING LIGHT AFFORDED US PROTECTION FROM THE WATCHFUL EYES AT SEA, BUT THE LIGHT OF DAY OBLITERATED OUR SAFEGUARD.

WE SUBMERGED.

MY BOOTS SLOSHED WITH WATER.

YOU MUST HAVE HAD THE DEVIL IN YOU...

THEY DROPPED AT LEAST TWENTY BOMBS.

WHO HAD CALLED TO ME IN THE NIGHT? WHO HAD SAVED ME?

LATER, AFTER THE ATTACK WAS OVER AND THE VALLEY TURNED INTO A SMOKING WILDERNESS, OTHER SOLDIERS WENT TO SEARCH FOR SURVIVORS. THERE WERE NONE.

I HAD MANY SIMILAR NEAR-DEATH EXPERIENCES, AND EACH BOLSTERED MY FAITH.

MANY DIED HORRIBLY AS WE RETREATED FROM THE ALLIES. WE DESTROYED BRIDGES AND TUNNELS IN OUR WAKE.

PALMI, THE STRAIGHT OF MESSINA, THE PLAINS OF SALERNO. FARTHER AND FARTHER NORTH.

NEAR MESSINA, WE WERE SHOT AT BY OUR ITALIAN ALLIES FOR THE FIRST TIME.

I DISTRIBUTED HOLY COMMUNION DAILY...

...TO BOTH SOLDIERS AND CIVILIANS, KILLED CASUALLY ON BOTH SIDES.

BETWEEN BANDAGES AND PERFORMING CRUDE SURGERY, I WOULD ASK, "ARE YOU CATHOLIC? HERE IS HOLY COMMUNION."

DECEMBER 7, ON LEAVE, I BECAME A SUB-DEACON.

DECEMBER 12, I WAS ORDAINED A DEACON.

NEW YEAR'S DAY, EN ROUTE BACK TO THE FRONT, I FOUND MYSELF IN ROME.

BY NOW, SOME COMBINATION OF SISTER SOLANA'S FAITH AND THE HORROR OF WAR CONVINCED ME OF THE RIGHTNESS OF MY QUEST.

THROUGH THE GENERAL OF THE FRANCISCAN ORDER AND A FRIEND AT THE GERMAN EMBASSY I WAS GRANTED AN UNLIKELY AUDIENCE WITH THE POPE.

MY PULSE THROBBED IN MY HEAD; DIZZY, I DROVE THROUGH THE GERMAN BLOCKADE INTO THE VATICAN.

1934

MY DESIRE TO BE ORDAINED CEMENTED WHEN I WAS A YOUNG MAN.

OUR CHRISTIAN MEETINGS WERE OUTLAWED SO WE MET IN SECRET.

WE WANTED TO PROVE THAT WE WERE BRAVE CHRISTIAN MEN.

THE POLICE CAUGHT US ON THE ROAD, AND WE WENT TO JUVENILE COURT...

...SO WE WENT DEEPER INTO THE BLACK FOREST ON OUR BICYCLES.

THE AUTHORITIES REJECTED CHRISTIANITY AND THE CATHOLIC CHURCH.

THEY REJECTED THEIR OWN HUMANITY AS WELL.

WHEN I WAS TWENTY-TWO, AND A SEMINARIAN, I WAS DRAFTED INTO THEIR RANKS.

I BECAME A COMPULSORY NAZI.

SINCE I HAD NO DESIRE TO BEAR ARMS, I EVENTUALLY TRANSFERRED TO THE MEDICAL CORPS.

I ANCHORED MYSELF TO CATHOLICISM FOR YEARS IN THE WEHRMACHT.

POPE PIUS XII

WE SPOKE FIRST OF OFFICIAL MATTERS, AND DEALT WITH THEM QUICKLY.

IS THERE ANYTHING ELSE?

FOR ONCE I HESITATED.

...I AM A MEDIC. I DO NOT KILL BUT TRY TO SAVE, BOTH BODY AND SOUL. THERE ARE NINE NEW GERMAN DIVISIONS, DYING WITHOUT A PRIEST TO HEAR THEIR CONFESSIONS.

I WOULD LIKE TO BE ORDAINED.

DO YOU HAVE A CERTIFICATE REGARDING YOUR STUDIES MY SON?

I DO NOT. BUT I CAN DISTRIBUTE THE EUCHARIST. I HAVE THE HOSTS IN MY POCKET. THE BISHOP OF PATTI GAVE ME SPECIAL PERMISSION.

I DID NOT MENTION MY LUGER'S ROLE IN THE MATTER.

DEAR BOY, THERE IS MORE TO IT...

IN THIS WAR YOU WOULD NOT BELIEVE WHAT ONE MORE PRIEST COULD ACCOMPLISH. MY PRESENCE IN THIS HATED COMPANY CAN BE A BLESSING.

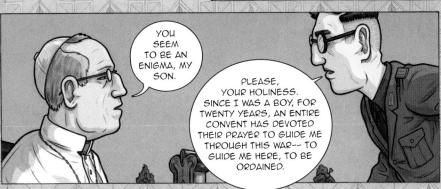

YOU SEEM TO BE AN ENIGMA, MY SON.

PLEASE, YOUR HOLINESS. SINCE I WAS A BOY, FOR TWENTY YEARS, AN ENTIRE CONVENT HAS DEVOTED THEIR PRAYER TO GUIDE ME THROUGH THIS WAR-- TO GUIDE ME HERE, TO BE ORDAINED.

... I WILL GRANT YOU THE DISPENSATION. YOU MAY ENTER THE PRIESTHOOD.

THAT DID IT.

BEFORE I COULD BE ORDAINED IN ROME, I WAS CALLED TO THE FRONT, TO MOUNTAINS SOUTH OF CASSINO.

THE DIOCESE THERE HAD BEEN A LITTLE GARDEN OF GOD, BUT, ALMOST OVERNIGHT, THE WAR DESTROYED EVERYTHING.

THE BUILDINGS WERE GONE, THE PEOPLE DEAD. ONLY THE MONASTERY REMAINED, ON THE DISTANT MOUNTAINTOP.

....
231.1...

THERE THE BISHOP OF CASSINO AGREED TO ORDAIN ME. WE WERE TO CELEBRATE THE SACRAMENT THE FOLLOWING DAY, UNSURE IF WE WOULD EVEN SURVIVE THAT LONG.

AT THAT TIME WE WERE DUG DEEP INTO THE MOUNTAINS—THE COLD OF FEBRUARY 1944.

WE HAD NO DOCTOR FOR WEEKS, AND IN THE CELLAR THAT WASN'T FULL OF SLEEPING TROOPS, I SET UP AND DID MY INADEQUATE BEST TO HELP THE WOUNDED.

...059.67-

THE DAY BEFORE THE PROPOSED ORDINATION, WE WERE IN A SMALL AREA NEAR MONTE CASSINO. IF I REMEMBER CORRECTLY, SAN GIORGIO. BACKED INTO THE WILDERNESS, WE FOUND AN OLD FARM CALLED MASSA CONSTANZA.

YOU FOOL! DON'T YOU THINK THE ENEMY HEARS THAT? YOU CAN'T JUST GIVE AWAY OUR POSITION!

UM...WHY? WHO CAN EAVESDROP ON US HERE IN THE MOUNTAINS?

ANYONE!

POK POK

BADAM

WSSHHH

HHHH

45

47

ONLY THIS SMALL CELLAR REMAINED INTACT.

OUTSIDE, EVERY TWO MINUTES THERE WAS A DOUBLE EXPLOSION; PAINED GROANS GREW WEAKER AND WEAKER.

WE FOUND THE LIEUTENANT HIDING IN A SHELL-HOLE.

ALL NIGHT, FAULBORN AND I SEARCHED OUTSIDE FOR THE WOUNDED.

THIS WAS REALITY: THE CRIES FOR HELP WHEN NONE COULD BE HAD!

THIS WAS EVIL; THIS WAS DARKNESS INCARNATE, AND I TREMBLED.

YOU WHO DWELL IN THE SHELTER OF THE MOST HIGH, WHO ABIDE IN THE SHADOW OF THE ALMIGHTY, SAY TO THE LORD: "MY REFUGE AND MY FORTRESS, MY GOD IN WHOM I TRUST." FOR HE WILL DELIVER YOU FROM THE SNARES OF THE HUNTERS, FROM THE DEADLY PLAGUE. HE WILL PROTECT YOU WITH HIS WINGS, AND YOU SHALL TAKE REFUGE BENEATH HIS WINGS: HIS FAITHFULNESS IS A SHIELD AND A BUCKLER. YOU SHALL NOT FEAR THE TERROR OF THE NIGHT NOR THE FLYING ARROW IN THE DAY; THE PLAGUE THAT WANDERS ABOUT IN THE NIGHT, NOR THE CALAMITY THAT DESTROYS AT NOON.

ABOUT IN THE NIGHT, ...AMITY THAT DESTROYS AT NOON. THOUGH A THOUSAND FALL AT YOUR SIDE AND TEN THOUSAND AT YOU... ...IGHT ...AND ... SHALL NOT C... ...NEAR ...HE HAS GIVEN HIS ANGEL ...HARGE OVER YOU

TO KEEP YOU IN ALL YOUR WAYS. IN THEIR HANDS SHALL THEY B...R YOU UP ...LEST YOU DASH YOUR FOOT AGAINST A STONE...

THE WORDS OF PSALM 91.

THE ANGELS WERE WITH ME.

THERE WERE VERY FEW TO BE BURIED; LITTLE MORE THAN PIECES... OF HUMAN BODIES.

SIR, THE SHELLS HAVE STOPPED.

WE SHOULD GO.

THE DREADFUL HARVEST OF WAR.

AFTER LENGTHY INTERROGATIONS, THE ALLIES ALLOWED ME TO CHOOSE A NEARBY PRISON CAMP AT A MONASTERY RUN BY FRANCISCANS.

SO I BECAME A PRISONER. THEY BROUGHT ME TO NAPLES, AND THEN TO A PLACE CALLED BIRKADEM, IN ALGERIA.

THE ARCHBISHOP OF ALGIERS INVESTIGATED ME AND EVENTUALLY MADE PLANS TO CELEBRATE HOLY ORDERS IN THE CAMP.

I ENTERED THE PRIESTHOOD JUNE 24TH, 1944.

THE BISHOP IMPOSED HIS HANDS ON ME, AND SISTER SOLANA MAY'S PREDICTION CAME TO PASS.

IN SEPTEMBER 1944, UNDER NEW SCRUTINY FROM THE FRENCH, I WAS TRANSFERRED TO AN INFAMOUS SOUTHERN PRISON NAMED KSAR ES SOUK IN MOROCCO.

BY THIS TIME GERMANY HAD LOST THE WAR AND A RIFT GREW AMONG THE CATHOLIC PRISONERS.

SOME REMAINED FAITHFUL TO THE IDEOLOGY OF THE NAZI PARTY.

OTHERS HATED THE NAZIS LIKE THE DEVIL BUT FEARED REPRISAL BACK IN GERMANY.

I SUPPORTED THE LATTER, AND, FOR THE FORMER, PRAYED FOR FORGIVENESS.

THIS DISCOMFORT, AND MY DESIRE TO CARRY OUT MY NEW DUTIES, MADE ME GLAD THAT I WAS SENT TO KSAR-ES-SOUK.

I BECAME THE PRIEST OF THE CAMP.

AT FIRST, LOCKED UP WITH THE OTHERS IN A ROOM, MISTRUST WAS A TANGIBLE THING.

THE ADAMANT NAZIS OPPOSED ME WITH VIOLENCE.

THOSE LOYAL TO HITLER BEAT HALF DEAD ANYONE WHO DARED TO DISAGREE WITH THEM. THE FRENCH GUARDS, TOO, ACTED AS CRUEL OVERLORDS.

BUT FOR A YEAR I DEFIANTLY PREACHED...

...AND SLOWLY I WAS ABLE TO BRING BLESSINGS TO ARID MEN.

LATER SOME BECAME PRIESTS; OTHER NON-CATHOLICS EMBRACED THE FAITH.

WE ARE GERMANS.

59

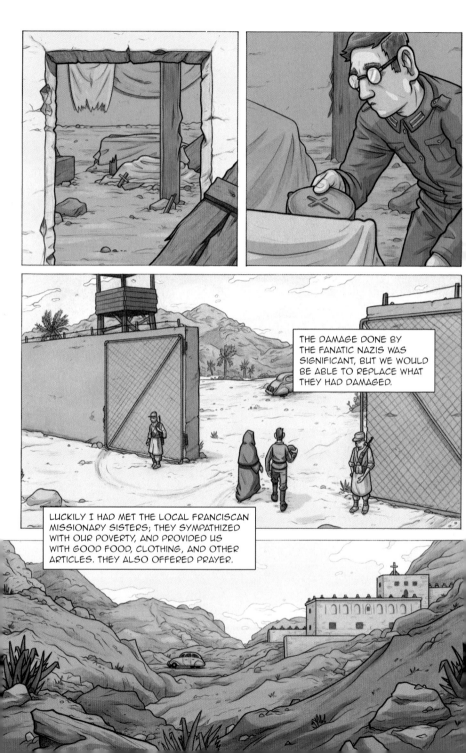

THE DAMAGE DONE BY THE FANATIC NAZIS WAS SIGNIFICANT, BUT WE WOULD BE ABLE TO REPLACE WHAT THEY HAD DAMAGED.

LUCKILY I HAD MET THE LOCAL FRANCISCAN MISSIONARY SISTERS; THEY SYMPATHIZED WITH OUR POVERTY, AND PROVIDED US WITH GOOD FOOD, CLOTHING, AND OTHER ARTICLES. THEY ALSO OFFERED PRAYER.

ESPECIALLY SISTER JEANNE.

SHE SPENT ALL HER TIME FASTING ALONE IN THIS VALLEY.

YOU MUST RETURN.

SISTER, I CANNOT. I HAVE FAILED TO BRING THAT CAMP TO CHRIST. THEY RESPOND WITH HATRED.

FATHER, IN GOD'S NAME, YOU ARE GOING BACK TO YOUR CAMP AT ONCE!

...

HERE. WRITE DOWN THE NAME OF THE WORST ENEMY OF THE CHURCH. NOW GO.

I DID, AND SISTER JEANNE PRAYED. FOR SIX HOURS, EVERY DAY, SHE PRAYED THAT KROCH WOULD CONVERT.

BUT AFTER MONTHS OF VIOLENCE BETWEEN US, I BEGAN TO ACCEPT OUR CONTINUAL OPPOSITION.

AK TAK TAK TA

KK RAK

THUD

KROCH?

I WAS A CATHOLIC, FATHER.

MY MOTHER WOULD BE SO PLEASED TO SEE ME IN THE CHURCH AGAIN.

WHEN KROCH CONVERTED THE MEN OF THE CAMP LINED UP FOR ME TO HEAR THEIR CONFESSIONS.

AGAIN PRAYER CARRIED ME. LIFE AS THE PRISON PRIEST BECAME A BLESSING.

KROCH PUBLICLY ACKNOWLEDGED HIS GUILT, ASKED TO BE PARDONED, AND RECEIVED THE SACRAMENT.

IN 1946 I WAS SENT BACK TO GERMANY. THE WAR, FOR ME, WAS OVER.

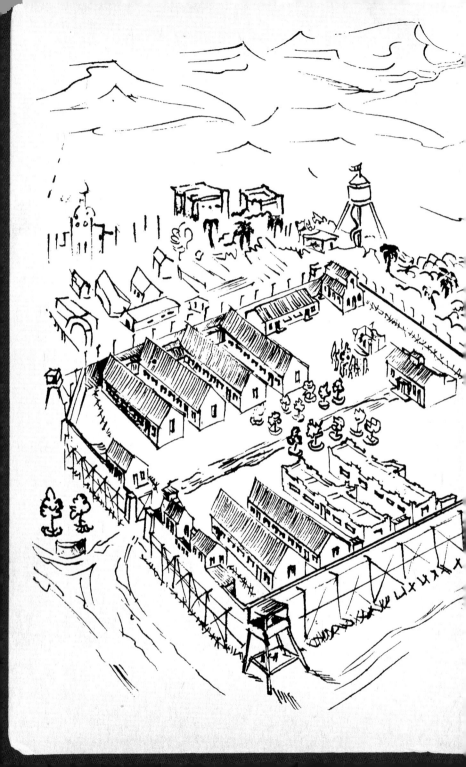

Epilogue

AFTER THE WAR

SAVED FROM EXECUTION

Although the war was over, some of Father Goldmann's most
difficult trials and challenges were still to come. Because
he had been a member of the SS, however unwillingly, the
French deemed him an enemy of France and transferred
him from Ksar-es-Souk—where Kroch had converted—to
a more severe prison camp in Meknes, a city in northern
Morocco. The judges in charge of his investigation began
to collect information and soon produced a list of twenty-
seven signatures from fellow prisoners of war, who claimed
Father Goldmann was one of the most dreaded and hated
Nazis in Germany. He was even falsely accused of being

the former commandant of Dachau, the Nazi concentration camp in southern Germany. The judges informed him that he was in danger of losing his life if the accusations were proven true. Aware of the seriousness of these charges, Father Goldmann defended himself, detailing his anti-Nazi activities in the war as well as his deeply held convictions. However, on February 27, 1946, he was informed that the court had found him guilty and that he would be executed the following day.

After a restless night, an officer came to his cell to escort him to the courtyard where he, along with other Germans convicted of war crimes, would face the firing squad. At that very moment, however, the officer hesitated and asked Father Goldmann to hear his confession. Father Goldmann advised him to go to one of the priests in town, but the officer insisted.

"No, no, it must be you," the officer protested, "because you will be going to heaven right away."

Unable to deny the officer's request, Father Goldmann heard his confession, after which the officer began to weep. He had become convinced of Father Goldmann's innocence, and it caused him great pain to have any part in the execution—but was equally convinced there was nothing he could do. Father Goldmann, who had two consecrated hosts with him, asked the officer if he would like to receive Holy Communion. The officer indicated he would, and devoutly received the Eucharist. At that moment, a French soldier entered the cell, waving a piece of paper and speaking excitedly to the officer. Both abruptly exited. Alone in his cell, Father Goldmann did not know what would happen next. Minutes later, rifle shots rang out from the courtyard. He had been spared from execution.

A few days later, Father Goldmann learned the reason for his reprieve. The Holy See had been informed of his predicament, and Pope Pius XII had personally intervened. Providentially, the French officer's request for confession had delayed the execution just long enough for the Pope's letter to arrive. God had saved him once again from near-certain death. Years later, Father Goldmann would learn just how providential the officer's request really was.

A PRISONER IN MOROCCO AND ALGERIA

Father Goldmann might have been spared death, but he was not a free man yet. Following his near execution, he was transferred to a prison camp south of Casablanca, Morocco where he would spend the next two months. Once again, he was informed that there were serious charges against him. In fact, his file had been marked "Nazi-priest," which caused the French guards to treat him harshly. To make matters worse, the conditions at the camp were truly horrific. Prisoners' rations were supplemented with the rats and snakes they caught to avoid starvation. Many were tortured to give up secrets they didn't have, and others made fraudulent charges against their fellow prisoners in exchange for extra rations.

Seeking to minister to the spiritual needs of the prisoners, Father Goldmann acquired some bread and wine and a small English missal for the celebration of Mass. In the middle of the night, a small group snuck out of the barracks to a nearby barn—the darkness broken only by the light of a small candle. They celebrated Mass in secret like this for two weeks, until the Holy Father intervened once again. He asked the French to treat Father Goldmann kindly, telling them that he had personally given permission for his ordination to the priesthood. In response, the commander of the prison camp allowed Father Goldmann to celebrate Mass in a small chapel that had been erected. This and other spiritual activities Father Goldmann performed did much to uplift the spirits of the men.

This "kind" treatment, however, was not to last. When a group of German soldiers escaped from the prison camp,

Father Goldmann was accused of assisting them. As a result, he was moved to another prison camp in Algeria where he was placed in barracks reserved for the most problematic prisoners of war—not run-of-the-mill German soldiers, but Nazi zealots. While he was not given any special treatment, the camp commander told him that he had the best protector in the world watching out for him—the Pope.

The conditions in this camp were much better than those in the previous one, and Father Goldmann renewed his prison ministry. He spent his days praying and tending to the spiritual needs of the prisoners, many of whom became upright Christians under his guidance. Other prisoners, who were not Catholic, came to embrace the Catholic Faith.

After several months, the camp commander informed Father Goldmann that the French no longer believed he was the Nazi they had once thought. They finally recognized that he wasn't masquerading as a priest to escape harsher punishment and that he had not been the former commandant of Dachau. Furthermore, the commander told him he would soon be released. It seemed that Father Goldmann's days as a prisoner of war were finally coming to an end.

As a first step toward his eventual release, Father Goldmann was sent to Paris. There he was assigned to a POW camp for seminarians who had been pressed into military service. He continued to minister to his fellow prisoners. He also was permitted to travel freely outside of the camp and took the opportunity to make pilgrimages to many of the great cathedrals and shrines of France. When he visited Lisieux, he said a special prayer of thanksgiving to St. Thérèse, whose special intercession he had requested when seeking the Pope's permission to be ordained.

RETURN TO THE FRANCISCAN LIFE

Following his official release in 1947, Father Goldmann returned to Fulda, the motherhouse of his Franciscan province in Germany, and reported to his religious superiors. Upon arriving, he was called in to speak with the prefect of studies, who informed him that his ordination had not been in accordance with the Franciscan statutes. He was told he would be treated as a newly ordained priest and could no longer hear confessions or preach sermons until he finished the required three-year course of studies. After ministering to countless souls as an ordained priest for nearly four years, often under peril of death, Father Goldmann was not delighted with the prospect of waiting another three years before once again exercising his full priestly faculties.

But Father Goldmann was used to overcoming setbacks, and so in obedience he pressed onward with characteristic faith and zeal. He devoted himself to his studies with such determination that, with the support and encouragement of kindly instructors, he completed three years of studies and passed his examinations in just nine months. With the requisite papers in hand, the shocked prefect of studies had no choice but to grant the veteran priest the return of his full priestly faculties. His studies complete, he could resume the care of souls.

For his first assignment, Father Goldmann was sent to assist a wise priest who was pastor of a parish in Fulda. This assignment helped Father Goldmann re-acclimate to civilian life. His priestly duties among the faithful were vastly different from those he had practiced on the battlefield and in the prison camps, and he learned much from the assignment. His difficulties were not completely behind him, though: American military authorities interrogated him nearly a dozen times for alleged Nazi activities during the war. Once again, Father Goldmann defended himself patiently, and, after revealing his involvement in the plot to assassinate Hitler, it was determined that he could not have been a true Nazi.

THE POWER OF PRAYER

Over the next few years, Father Goldmann was assigned to work with seminarians in Germany and Holland. Wherever his duties took him, he would visit all the different monasteries and convents in the surrounding area. On one such trip to the south of Germany, he stopped by the Franciscan Motherhouse at Siessen, where he was introduced to a sister whose face bore the strain of many years of intense suffering. Yet she herself radiated serenity and joy. During his visit, birds came fluttering in through her window as she called them by name. Speaking with her and the other sisters, Father Goldmann learned that she had been bedridden for twenty years, and that throughout this time she had offered up all of her suffering for his vocation to the priesthood. God had accepted the sister's suffering and prayers just as he had accepted the supplications of Sister Solana May.

He also learned of another incredible testament to the power of prayer on a visit to the Sisters of Perpetual Adoration in Grimmenstein, Switzerland. They related that when he had been sentenced to death in the French prison camp, a French officer, believing in his innocence, had asked the sisters to pray for him. They did so in a cycle of perpetual adoration before the Blessed Sacrament—a cycle unbroken until they learned of his reprieve. They even showed him his name, which had been written on a card and placed on a kneeler in front of the Blessed Sacrament. Father Goldmann was taken aback. His reprieve from execution had been truly providential, and he came to understand even more how God had been watching over him, even in the darkest moments. The words of Scripture had been fulfilled: that whoever prays to the Father in the name of the Son will be heard.

A MISSIONARY IN JAPAN

For many years, Father Goldmann had harbored a great desire to go to Japan as a missionary. Upon receiving word that his visa had been approved, he wasted no time in making the necessary arrangements and was soon on his way. In a letter dated January 22, 1954, written while flying over India and Burma en route to Bangkok, the enthusiastic missionary described this great adventure:

> Forests, jungle, swamps. No settlement for miles and miles. In clear weather, from a height of twenty thousand feet, one can see large areas of mighty river valleys, a vast expanse. And then the inhabitants! Each people is different.... What an immense mission field here! But that is what we are here for. I hope for the best.

Father Goldmann arrived in Tokyo on January 25, 1954, the feast of the conversion of St. Paul. The capital of Germany's

wartime ally, still recovering from aerial bombardment, was sheathed in ice and snow. Looking out upon this frozen landscape, Father Goldmann thought of all the souls needing a spiritual springtime—souls just waiting to be "thawed out by the warmth of God's grace and illumined by the fire of the Holy Spirit." As much as Father Goldmann wanted to immerse himself in ministry, however, he first had to pass a steep cultural learning curve. Describing his initial impressions and hardships, he wrote:

> I am at school, studying hard. The language is unbelievably difficult, harder than any I have learned so far…. My bed is Asiatic, a few blankets on the floor. By evening I am worn out from the most intense study. Of thousands of written characters to be memorized, I know only 45, the easiest [ones] at that…. Our parish counts three hundred thousand [non-Christians] and one hundred Christians—no lack of work. These few Christians, however, are unbelievably zealous. As many as forty at a time squeeze into my thirteen-by-nineteen-foot room, which serves as a chapel as well. The people are exceedingly poor but most lovable.

Indeed, poverty was rampant in the Tokyo neighborhood in which he served as pastor of St. Elizabeth's Church. From the start, Father Goldmann set about attending to the physical and material needs of the people as well as providing for their spiritual needs. His charitable efforts gave rise to the "Ragpicker's Student Aid Fund." Each day, Father Goldmann would rummage through garbage bins to collect bottles, paper, tin cans, and anything else of value, which he then sold. He managed to collect enough money to cover the schooling expenses for some one hundred students. To alleviate the cramped living conditions in which most people found themselves—large families often squeezed together in single-room homes constructed of bamboo and paper—he began a housing fund. As a result of his charitable efforts he started attracting converts. In the first few months, thirty-eight of his new neighbors sought Baptism.

Father Goldmann also recognized another need. Because of their stifling poverty, many people in his

parish never enjoyed the chance to venture beyond their own neighborhood and experience the rest, joy, and beauty of nature. To remedy this, he decided to build a home in the mountains so that mothers and children could enjoy short vacations. (The men, unfortunately, had to remain in the city and work.) Seeking property on which to build his mountain home, Father Goldmann solicited the aid of a wealthy but notoriously stingy businessman. As the priest expected, the businessman angrily rebuffed him, even swearing never to give him any property. Father Goldmann prayed for St. Anthony's intercession, promising that if it were successful, the retreat house would bear his name. After cooling off, the hot-headed businessman experienced a miraculous change of heart and donated the property that came to be called St. Anthony's Home in the Mountains.

In the years that followed, Father Goldmann not only met the financial needs of his own parish of St. Elizabeth's but helped build a second parish, St. Joseph the Worker, as well as a mission parish. He also founded a hospital. Although poor themselves, his parishioners adopted an even needier sister parish in India and donated what they could to alleviate the plight of their brothers and sisters in Christ. In time, through the efforts of Father Goldmann and his flock, enough funds were raised to build eight new Indian parishes, a seminary, an orphanage, several schools, and a modern hospital. In the meantime, the Catholics of Japan, whose numbers included ever more converts, continued to thrive spiritually as well as materially as their war-torn country recovered. God, they learned, would not be outdone in generosity.

THE FINAL YEARS

For twenty-two years Father Goldmann continued his work as a parish priest in Tokyo, preaching, according to his own count, a total of forty thousand sermons throughout the Land of the Rising Sun. Seventeen times he led Japanese Catholics on pilgrimages to the Holy Land, staying only in monasteries and following the rigorous Spiritual

Exercises of St. Ignatius of Loyola. After helping found two Carmelite monasteries in India and several more in Japan, he then founded the Academy of Ecclesiastical Music in Tokyo. For the first fifteen years he directed the school, whose reputation has garnered world-wide acclaim.

Father Goldmann's mission to Japan, which would span four decades, began in poverty but ended in spiritual riches. Even the highest authorities recognized his wondrous works. For his humanitarian efforts, Emperor Hirohito made Father Goldmann a member of the Order of Good Deeds, the highest award bestowed by the state for social work.

Yet, the years had taken a toll on Father Goldmann. He developed a chronic health condition and suffered two heart attacks. After suffering his third in 1994, doctors pronounced him dead at first. But God was not through with him just yet. He awoke from a coma and returned to recuperate in Germany, where, except for several trips, including one to Japan, he remained for the rest of his life.

In his twilight years Father Goldmann enjoyed a peacefully structured existence in what he termed, although not literally, "absolute quiet." Rising at five, his days were filled with studying, personally replying to the many thousands of letters and cards sent to him, and receiving numerous visitors from all over the world. Father Goldmann also spent five to six hours a day in prayer, never forgetting that it was God, not he, who had accomplished so much with one life. When Father Goldmann toured the United States many years earlier, the speeches he gave about his World War II experiences were recorded and formed the basis of a book that has now been translated into more than a dozen languages. Father Goldmann touched many lives by his ministries and, through the telling of his amazing story, continues to do so.

Father Goldmann departed this life from the Franciscan monastery in Fulda on July 26, 2003. The odyssey that was his life—so full of unexpected twists and turns—is a timeless testimony to the power and providence of God, who guides all who take shelter in the shadow of his wings.

Patti 4 ag[...]

In linea eccezionale e [...]
facoltà straordinarie, [...]
ricevuto dalla S. Sede, [...]
ai chierici cattolici della
divisione tedesca dei carri [...]
di portare con la debita [...]
la S. Comunione ai loro co[...]
e specialmente ai feriti[...]

+ Angelo [...]

Quod ad me attinet et meam Dioecesim [...]
confirmo facultates extraordinarias supra d[...]
Mura[...] in Lucania die 20 septembris [...]
+ Bartholomaeus Mangino

Photographs

THE LIFE OF
FATHER GOLDMANN

Born October 10, 1916, young Karl Goldmann
was twelve years old when this photograph
was taken.

When Karl's mother died in 1924, Sister Solana May told him, "I will take the place of your mother." She was to carry out her promise in a remarkable way. Sister is shown with Karl (far right) and three other altar boys whom she trained.

In September 1926, Karl served in a work camp of the
Arbeitsdienst on the Lüneberger Heath. For the first time he
learned what life was to be like in de-Christianized Germany.
Karl's height makes him stand out from his fellow workers.

In October 1936, Karl became
a novice at the Franciscan
novitiate at Gorheim.

From Gorheim, he was sent back to
Fulda, where he studied philosophy for
two years. This photograph shows the
entrance to the Frauenberg cloister.

On August 28, 1939, these young Franciscan seminarians
were notified that they were to be inducted into the
army. Karl (Frater Gereon to his brothers in St. Francis)
is in the third row, third from the right.

This picture shows Karl in late 1943 during the Italian campaign, twenty-seven years old, a hardened veteran non-combatant often finding himself bolstering the courage of faint-hearted officers even younger than himself.

Sent to desolate country near the Polish border, the men dubbed their base "Camp Earthworm." Here Karl marches head and shoulders above his comrades in the communications platoon of the SS, to which he was assigned.

In the winter, despite the fact that the seminarians were exhausted from drilling, they went to a Catholic church in nearby Bürschen for prayer and meditation. Of the eleven seminarians in Karl's platoon, the only one to give up his faith was the man who refused to pray each evening.

Partially obscured by the antenna of his equipment,
Karl and a fellow seminarian learn radio operation
in the field.

After a period of maneuvers in early 1940, Heinrich Himmler
visited the men at Camp Earthworm. Struck by the courage of the
seminarians, who refused to compromise their ideals of faith,
Himmler gave them permission to carry out their religious
duties without interference from the hostile anti-Christian
officers of the SS.

....eim. Blick auf die Hauptstraße

In the spring of 1940, Karl's unit was sent to the village of
Herbolzheim, near the Rhine.

At Les Islettes, the Germans came upon the graves of their
predecessors killed during World War I. In the background, the
bombarded town is in flames.

Here his memorial catafalque stands
before the empty altar he served.

Priests, treated as ordinary civilians by the Nazi regime, were
inducted into the army as common soldiers. Here a man of God
lies in an anonymous grave.

Karl did his best to commandeer food from German supply dumps
in order to feed the starving French children.

In pursuit of the fleeing French, the German forces sometimes
had to travel forty-five to fifty miles a day.

After completing officer's training, Karl
was called upon to renounce his faith.
He refused and was expelled from the SS.
This photo, taken in May 1941, is his last
in the SS uniform.

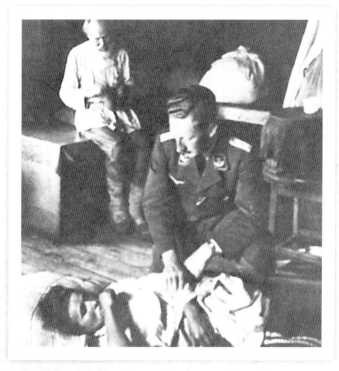

Receiving medical training at the Russian front, Karl cared
for the wounded through the winter of 1942. Then, perhaps
fortunately, he contracted dysentery and was invalided to
southern Germany.

Scorning the cross of Christianity, these Germans rest in death beneath the "rune of the dead," a pagan symbol adopted by fervent Nazis.

After the trial, he was permitted to study at Freiburg in September 1942.

A common grave of thirty-seven SS soldiers. Here they repose, not under the cross of Christ, but under the rune of death.

In an audience with Pope Pius XII on January 3, 1944, Karl was given a note permitting him to be ordained a priest—despite the fact that he had not completed his studies.

Most Holy Father,

Fr. Gereon Goldmann, deacon of the Franciscan
province of Thuringia, prostrate at the feet of Your
Holiness, humbly begs:

1) A dispensation of one year and six months
lacking in theological studies, so that he can be ordained
priest.

2) That any bishop can ordain him priest, on any
day, because of extraordinary reasons.

And may God etc......

In audience with the Holy Father, 10 January, 1944.

His Holiness Pope Pius XII, referring the matter to
the below-mentioned Secretary of the Sacred Congregation
in charge of matters pertaining to Religious Societies,
graciously grants all the favors requested, together with
the faculty of hearing the confessions of the Military
alone, having placed the serious responsibility on the
conscience of the Superiors.

Notwithstanding anything.

Given in Rome, day, month and year as above.

Sent back to Europe, where the war prisoners were
to be given their freedom, Father Goldmann assisted
at Mass celebrated at a prisoners' camp in Chartres
by the Papal Nuncio, Cardinal Roncalli—later Pope
John XXIII. This took place in 1947.

Cardinal Roncalli celebrating Mass. Father Goldmann is
third from the right—the tallest, as usual.

After completing his studies, Father Goldmann
served in parishes in Germany and the Netherlands.
Here he leads a band of pilgrims to the Shrine of the
Precious Blood at Waldurn.

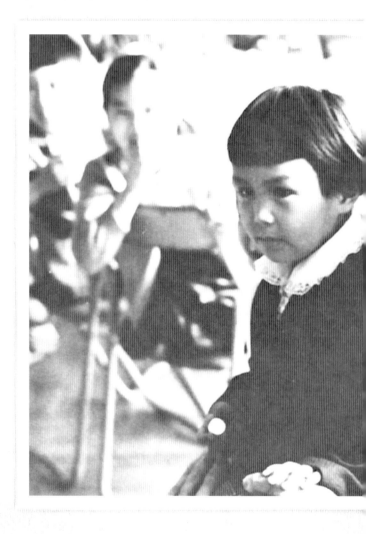

When he was an altar boy, Father Goldmann had dreamed of being a missionary in Japan. His dream came true in 1954, when he was sent to Tokyo.

Father Goldmann celebrating Mass for his Japanese congregation.

Mission Station Bibai with kindergarten and Sisters' convent.

Pilgrim group in an audience with Pope Paul VI in Rome.

Christmas 1965: Father Goldmann received
the highest decoration the state awards
for social welfare work—the Order of
Good Deeds—in the temple of Jeiji, Tokyo.

A Word from the Author and Illustrator

MAX TEMESCU

It has been several months since I drew this comic and even longer since I wrote the script. To go heavily into the process of making the book or to delve into the thematic content here would probably be a mistake. It has been long enough since the ideas on these pages had a full grip on my mind that commenting substantially on this book would provide a lousy armature constructed out of hazy memories and unfocussed ideas. Given that, there are just a couple of quick thoughts that might elucidate my relationship to this comic as its coauthor.

This is Goldmann's story; despite the immensity of his situation, this is a story about Goldmann. The words are taken almost entirely from his own first-hand account of what happened to him in his early life through World War II. It lacks the grandeur and seeming objectivity that many war stories, especially those set in World War II, often possess. It also lacks a full description of the context in which Goldmann lived his life. That context, the one that is frequently used as the majestic backdrop for heroic and harrowing war stories, is not something that Goldmann ever experienced. It is something ineffable that he, selectively, was trying to parse. I encourage anybody interested in Goldmann's life to learn more about the substrate that 1940's Europe provided him.

Having read through some of the historical facts and reports occurring around Goldmann's situation, I am impressed by the fact that anybody emerged functioning from the war. Of course the Holocaust and the brutality of the eastern theater stand out as some of the most significant atrocities of modern times, but the absolute pervasiveness of people doing massive, terrible things is mind numbing. Goldmann's story is interesting to me because it is mundane.

It is about a man cleaving manageable handfuls of shale off the mountains of horror that surrounded him and squeezing.

More important than that interest in this story, though, is Goldmann himself. Inextricably linked to his Franciscan beliefs, Goldmann's faith and his relationship to God were by his account the most important factor in his relationship to the awfulness of the war. I do not share Goldmann's faith, but I cannot deny that it manifested tangibly in his life. His beliefs were central to his life and it felt important to avoid separating Goldmann from his religion despite

"his relationship to God... the most important factor in his relationship to the awfulness of the war."

our difference of opinion on the matter, because he was so solidly fused with it through the battles and bombings. Applied broadly this means I took him as he presented himself. I encourage anybody reading either this book or its source to do the same: listen to Goldmann as purely as possible, at least at first, regardless of affiliations.

Goldmann's story is an interesting one. It is about a person in a unique situation. A horrible, unique situation. As a result, Goldmann's story is not an average war story, and I value its difference.

MAX TEMESCU
October 8, 2015
New York City

The Making of
Shadow of his Wings

SCRIPT & SKETCHES

14B.5

INT. EVENING. GOLDMANN sits in a train almost full of soldiers. The seat next to him is unoccupied, and he reads his small bible. Through the window behind him a tuscan hillside streaks by.

>CAPTION
>>We passed Rome a few days later. Perhaps Solana May's faith was not so childish.

PAGE 15

15.1

EXT. DUSK. Through a stone archway GOLDMANN and FAULBORN walk across a cobbled courtyard. Behind them there is a tranquil sea.

>CAPTION
>>After the unit was decimated they fell back. I found them setting up defenses near Patti, just off the Italian mainland.
>>
>>After three days there, we had more than four hundred dead and wounded.

15.2

Large aerial shot of the courtyard. GOLDMANN and FAULBORN are walking away from their ambulance. Its doors are still open. They are walking toward three figures seated around wooden table in the corner of the courtyard. The courtyard is outside a simple cathedral at the top of a shrub covered mountain; it has a flat stone facade and a base made out of roughly hewn rocks. Periodically tropical looking trees show through the shrubbery on the mountain, along with ascending slanted roofs and a winding dirt road.

>CAPTION
>>An injured friend, knowing I spoke Italian, asked me to get a local priest to bring Holy Communion to save the souls of our dying men.
>>
>>Ever faithful Private Faulborn agreed to drive me.

15.3

GOLDMANN and FAULBORN reach the seated figures. All three are distinctly different, but also distinctly old white men. The man in the middle, the BISHOP OF PATTI, is particularly old and white; his face is heavily stubbled, he is large, and he is very dirty. On their janky wooden table there is a torn up old map of the area covered in pebbles arranged in formations and couple spyglasses.

125

SoHW

126